TEAM SPIRIT ®

SMART BOOKS FOR YOUNG FANS

THE NEW YORK YANKEES

BY
MARK STEWART

NORWOODHOUSE PRESS
CHICAGO, ILLINOIS

Norwood House Press
P.O. Box 316598
Chicago, Illinois 60631

For information regarding Norwood House Press, please visit our website at:
www.norwoodhousepress.com or call 866-565-2900.

All photos courtesy of Getty Images except the following:
SportsChrome (4, 10, 12, 14, 19, 32), Goudey Gum Co. (6, 17, 20), Exhibit Supply Co. (7),
Associated Press (9), The Daily News (15, 31),
Author's Collection (16, 24, 34 top and bottom left, 36, 37), Topps, Inc. (21, 22, 25, 34 bottom right),
Black Book Partners Archives (23, 35 top right & bottom, 38, 39, 40, 45),
Famous Publications (27 inset), Official Magazine Corp. (35 top left), TCMA, Ltd. (41),
General Mills (42), Matt Richman (48).
Cover Photo: SportsChrome

The memorabilia and artifacts pictured in this book are presented for educational and informational purposes,
and come from the collection of the author.

Editor: Mike Kennedy
Designer: Ron Jaffe
Project Management: Black Book Partners, LLC.
Special thanks to Topps, Inc.

Library of Congress Cataloging-in-Publication Data

Stewart, Mark, 1960-
  The New York Yankees / by Mark Stewart. -- Library ed.
    p. cm. -- (Team spirit)
  Includes bibliographical references and index.
  Summary: "A Team Spirit Baseball edition featuring the New York Yankees
that chronicles the history and accomplishments of the team. Includes access
to the Team Spirit website, which provides additional information, updates
and photos"--Provided by publisher.
  ISBN 978-1-59953-490-9 (library : alk. paper) -- ISBN 978-1-60357-370-2
(ebook) 1. New York Yankees (Baseball team)--History--Juvenile literature.
I. Title.
  GV875.N4S74 2012
  796.357'64097471--dc23
                                        2011048489

Manufactured in the United States of America in North Mankato, Minnesota.
196N—012012

COVER PHOTO: The Yankees can barely contain their joy after their 2009 championship.

TABLE OF CONTENTS

CHAPTER	PAGE
MEET THE YANKEES	4
GLORY DAYS	6
HOME TURF	12
DRESSED FOR SUCCESS	14
WE WON!	16
GO-TO GUYS	20
CALLING THE SHOTS	24
ONE GREAT DAY	26
LEGEND HAS IT	28
IT REALLY HAPPENED	30
TEAM SPIRIT	32
TIMELINE	34
FUN FACTS	36
TALKING BASEBALL	38
GREAT DEBATES	40
FOR THE RECORD	42
PINPOINTS	44
GLOSSARY	46
EXTRA INNINGS	47
INDEX	48

ABOUT OUR GLOSSARY

In this book, there may be several words that you are reading for the first time. Some are sports words, some are new vocabulary words, and some are familiar words that are used in an unusual way. All of these words are defined on page 46. Throughout the book, sports words appear in **bold type**. Regular vocabulary words appear in ***bold italic type***.

MEET THE YANKEES

Sports teams usually are judged by one thing: championships. The New York Yankees have more championships than any sports team in North America. From 1923 to 2009, they won the **American League (AL)** crown 40 times. During that same period, the Yankees captured 27 **World Series** championships.

For a team to have this kind of success, it must have a winning *tradition* and a winning attitude. Of course, it also helps to have great players. Sometimes the Yankees get them as teenagers and bring them up through the **minor leagues**. Sometimes the Yankees find them on other teams.

This book tells the story of the Yankees. They play in a city filled with fans who expect them to win every year. The Yankees don't mind the pressure. In fact, they demand nothing less of themselves.

The Yankees celebrate a victory during the 2010 season. The players and fans begin each year expecting nothing less than a championship.

GLORY DAYS

The Yankees were one of eight teams to join the American League when it began play in 1901. Only they weren't called the Yankees, and they didn't play in New York. For their first two seasons, the team was called the Baltimore Orioles. In 1903, they moved to New York and became the Highlanders. Not until 1913 did the team change its name to Yankees.

SPORT KINGS GUM
BABE RUTH

New York's first stars were pitchers Jack Chesbro, Russ Ford, and Slim Caldwell. New York became known for its hitting in 1920, after the team made a deal with the Boston Red Sox for Babe Ruth. Unlike the other hitters of his day, Ruth swung hard at every pitch that looked good. When he connected, the ball traveled higher and farther than anyone had ever seen. Ruth would go on to set records with 60 homers in a season and 714 in his career.

Ruth changed the game with his power hitting. The Yankees built a championship club around him. When New York added

LEFT: Babe Ruth
RIGHT: This postcard shows New York's four team leaders from the 1930s—Tony Lazzeri, Lefty Gomez, Lou Gehrig, and Joe DiMaggio.

Lou Gehrig to the lineup, the team was just about unbeatable. Ruth and Gehrig got plenty of help from dangerous hitters such as Bob Meusel, Earle Combs, and Tony Lazzeri. New York's pitching was almost as good. The Yankees won the **pennant** six times during the 1920s and added three World Series championships.

Gehrig was the heart of the team in the 1930s. A graceful young star named Joe DiMaggio joined him in 1936. The "Yankee Clipper" chased down balls in center field and always seemed to get a hit in the **clutch**. The Yankees won five World Series during the *decade*. Among their stars were Lefty Gomez, Red Ruffing, and Bill Dickey. DiMaggio played through the 1940s, when the Yankees won four more championships.

Having big stars play for many years was the key to success for New York. In 1951, DiMaggio played his final season. That same year, Mickey Mantle was called up from the minors. Mantle was the

greatest **switch-hitter** the game had ever seen. Some said he hit the ball even harder than Ruth had.

Mantle was the heart of a club that won 12 pennants and seven World Series from 1951 to 1964. His teammates included Yogi Berra, Phil Rizzuto, Whitey Ford, Elston Howard, and Roger Maris. The Yankees always did a good job of finding reliable **role players** who fit in well with their superstar teammates.

New York's magic touch began to fade in 1965. For the first time since their early years, the Yankees went more than 10 seasons without a first-place finish. The team needed a boost of energy. It got it when George Steinbrenner became the Yankees' owner in 1973. Steinbrenner loved to win—and he hated to lose even more. The "Boss" rebuilt the Yankees around catcher Thurman Munson and outfielder Reggie Jackson. The two stars didn't always get along, but together they led New York to championships in 1977 and 1978.

LEFT: Yogi Berra and Mickey Mantle   **ABOVE**: George Steinbrenner chats with Joe Torre. The Boss hired Torre as the team's manager in 1996.

The Yankees continued to put good players on the field in the 1980s, including Dave Winfield, Don Mattingly, and Dave Righetti. However, New York would not return to the top of baseball until 1996. That season, manager Joe Torre led the Yankees to their first championship in nearly two decades. The team relied on a core of exciting young players, including Derek Jeter, Bernie Williams, Jorge Posada, Tino Martinez, Paul O'Neill, Andy Pettitte, and Mariano Rivera.

This group of Yankees reminded fans of New York's championship teams of the past. Jeter was their leader. He had a knack for making big plays when the pressure was on. Rivera was just as important. Many considered him the best relief pitcher in baseball history.

The Yankees made it to the **playoffs** each year from 1995 to 2007. Along the way they won four World Series. Every season, a new hero would step forward. Some were young, such as Alfonso Soriano and

ABOVE: Derek Jeter   **RIGHT**: Mariano Rivera

Robinson Cano. Others were experienced players added in trades or signed as **free agents**. That list included Wade Boggs, Mike Mussina, Roger Clemens, Alex Rodriguez, and Jason Giambi.

In 2009, the Yankees won their 27th championship. As in seasons past, the stars of the team were a mix of young and old. Jeter was still going strong. The same was true of Posada, Rivera, and Pettitte. New players such as CC Sabathia and Mark Teixeira had joined the club. Hideki Matsui, an aging Japanese star in his final season with the team, was the hero of the World Series. In the years that followed, the Yankees continued their tradition of mixing youth with experience. Although the names and faces changed, every Opening Day seemed like old times again.

HOME TURF

W hen Yankee Stadium opened in 1923, it was the most fantastic sports stadium in America. Some called it a "*cathedral* of baseball." The stadium was built to give an advantage to left-handed sluggers. Yankee Stadium was modernized in the 1970s. A group of monuments honoring the team's great players that had been on the field was moved behind the left field wall.

In 2009, the Yankees opened a new Yankee Stadium. It was built across the street from the site of the old ballpark. From the inside, the field and stands look almost identical to the old stadium. The monuments were brought over from the old stadium, too. From the outside, the stadium is similar to the old one with its limestone-and-concrete design.

BY THE NUMBERS

- The Yankees' stadium has 50,291 seats.
- The distance from home plate to the left field foul pole is 318 feet.
- The distance from home plate to the center field wall is 408 feet.
- The distance from home plate to the right field foul pole is 314 feet.

The Yankees host the Philadelphia Phillies in their new stadium during the 2009 World Series.

DRESSED FOR SUCCESS

The Yankees' uniform may be the most famous in baseball. The team has been wearing dark blue *pinstripes* since 1912. They have used the *NY logo* on their hats since 1909. A larger version of this logo has been used on the uniform top since 1936. Over the next 70 years, New York's uniform changed very little.

The Yankees wear their pinstripes at home and a gray uniform with *New York* across the chest on the road. They have pulled on solid blue socks for more than 90 years. The Yankees' *NY* can be found on hats and shirts in almost every country in the world. When the team signed Hideki Matsui in 2003, stores in Tokyo sold out of Yankees merchandise in a few days.

LEFT: CC Sabathia delivers a pitch wearing the team's famous pinstripes in a 2011 game.　　**ABOVE**: Bill Dickey wears the home pinstripes during spring training 70 years earlier.

WE WON!

In 2009, the Yankees won the 40th pennant in their history. No team in either league has come close to that record of success. Choosing the greatest Yankees team is almost impossible. For example, the Yankees of the 1920s won six pennants in eight years. They were led by great hitters such as Babe Ruth, Lou Gehrig, Bob Meusel, Earle Combs, and Tony Lazzeri. Waite Hoyt, Herb Pennock, and Bob Shawkey took care of the pitching. The Yankees won the World Series in 1923, 1927, and 1928.

The Yankees teams of the 1930s and early 1940s were even more successful. They won eight pennants in 12 years and were the best team in baseball. Those teams had hitting stars such as Gehrig, Bill Dickey, Charlie Keller, Joe Gordon, and Tommy Henrich. Their pitching

LEFT: Bob Meusel, Babe Ruth, and Earle Combs
RIGHT: Lefty Gomez

was led by Red Ruffing, Lefty Gomez, Johnny Murphy, and Spud Chandler. The biggest star of this period was Joe DiMaggio, who joined the team in 1936. In 1941, he set a record by reaching base on a hit in 56 games in a row. The Yankees won the World Series seven times from 1932 to 1943, including four in a row from 1936 to 1939.

In the years after **World War II**, the Yankees were the best team in baseball again. From 1947 to 1964, they won the pennant in all but three seasons. The team's pitching staff was excellent. It was led by Allie Reynolds, Vic Raschi, Joe Page, Eddie Lopat, Whitey Ford, and Bob Turley. These teams also starred great hitters, including Bobby Richardson, Yogi Berra, Phil Rizzuto, Billy Martin, Bill Skowron, Elston Howard, Roger Maris, and Mickey Mantle. During this era, the Yankees won the World Series 10 times—including five in a row from 1949 to 1953. Their most dramatic championship came in 1958,

when they defeated the Milwaukee Braves after trailing in the World Series three games to one.

The Yankees returned to power again in the 1970s. They captured the pennant four times from 1976 to 1981, and won the World Series in 1977 and 1978. The stars of these teams included Thurman Munson, Graig Nettles, Reggie Jackson, Mickey Rivers, Lou Piniella, Willie Randolph, Chris Chambliss, Ron Guidry, and Goose Gossage.

Yet another group of stars led the Yankees to the top of baseball starting in the mid-1990s.

Paul O'Neill, Bernie Williams, Derek Jeter, Jorge Posada, Mariano Rivera, and Andy Pettitte made up the heart of a club that captured six pennants from 1996 to 2003. The Yankees won the World Series in 1996 and three times in a row from 1998 to 2000.

Jeter, Posada, Rivera, and Pettitte were on the team in 2009 when the Yankees returned to the World Series. They teamed up with new stars Mark Teixeira, Robinson Cano, Alex Rodriguez, and CC Sabathia to defeat the Philadelphia Phillies. It marked the 27th time the Yankees were World Series champions.

LEFT: Thurman Munson drills a hit to left field.   **ABOVE**: The Yankees celebrate their championship in 2000 over the New York Mets.

GO-TO GUYS

To be a true star in baseball, you need more than a quick bat and a strong arm. You have to be a "go-to guy"—someone the manager wants on the pitcher's mound or in the batter's box when it matters most. Fans of the Yankees have had a lot to cheer about over the years, including these great stars …

THE PIONEERS

BABE RUTH   Outfielder

• BORN: 2/6/1895 • DIED: 8/16/1948 • PLAYED FOR TEAM: 1920 TO 1934

Babe Ruth was the greatest slugger in baseball history. He had the personality to match his *majestic* home runs. When the Yankees opened Yankee Stadium in 1923, people called it the "House That Ruth Built."

LOU GEHRIG   First Baseman

• BORN: 6/19/1903 • DIED: 6/2/1941
• PLAYED FOR TEAM: 1923 TO 1939

Lou Gehrig was a line drive machine, spraying hits all over the field—including 493 home runs. He was tough, too. Gehrig played 2,130 games in a row.

ABOVE: Lou Gehrig   **RIGHT**: Whitey Ford

JOE DIMAGGIO   Outfielder

- BORN: 11/25/1914   • DIED: 3/8/1999
- PLAYED FOR TEAM: 1936 TO 1942 & 1946 TO 1951

Joe DiMaggio was the best all-around player to wear a Yankees uniform. He was the league's best hitter, baserunner, and fielder during the 1930s.

JOE GORDON   Second Baseman

BORN: 2/18/1915   • DIED: 4/14/1978   • PLAYED FOR TEAM: 1938 TO 1943 & 1946

Joe Gordon was an **All-Star** every season he played for the Yankees. In 2009, he was elected to the **Hall of Fame**.

YOGI BERRA   Catcher

- BORN: 5/12/1925   • PLAYED FOR TEAM: 1946 TO 1963

Yogi Berra was one of baseball's greatest clutch hitters. If the Yankees needed a hit late in a game, there was no one they would rather send to bat.

WHITEY FORD   Pitcher

- BORN: 10/21/1928   • PLAYED FOR TEAM: 1950 TO 1967

Whitey Ford was the Yankees' ace for more than 10 seasons. He won the **Cy Young Award** in 1961.

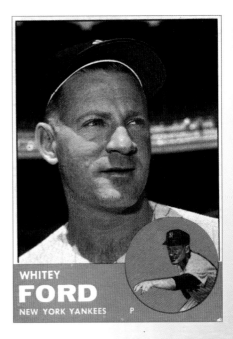

WHITEY
FORD
NEW YORK YANKEES   P

MICKEY MANTLE   Outfielder

- BORN: 10/20/1931   • DIED: 8/13/1995
- PLAYED FOR TEAM: 1951 TO 1968

Mickey Mantle was the most powerful switch-hitter in history. He hit more long home runs than anyone during the 1950s and 1960s.

MODERN STARS

THURMAN MUNSON
Catcher

• BORN: 6/7/1947 • DIED: 8/2/1979 • PLAYED FOR TEAM: 1969 TO 1979

Thurman Munson was the leader of the Yankees during the 1970s. He won the **Most Valuable Player (MVP)** Award in 1976. Munson was killed in a plane crash three years later.

REGGIE JACKSON
Outfielder

• BORN: 5/18/1946 • PLAYED FOR TEAM: 1977 TO 1981

Reggie Jackson loved to be in the spotlight. He played his best in the playoffs and earned the nickname "Mr. October." Jackson hit 12 home runs in 34 **postseason** games as a Yankee.

DON MATTINGLY
First Baseman

• BORN: 4/20/1961 • PLAYED FOR TEAM: 1982 TO 1995

Don Mattingly was the team's best player for nearly 10 years. The fans called him "Donnie Baseball" because he loved the game so much. Mattingly was an All-Star six times and won eight **Gold Gloves**.

BERNIE WILLIAMS
Outfielder

• BORN: 9/13/1968 • PLAYED FOR TEAM: 1991 TO 2006

Bernie Williams played center field for the Yankees longer than Joe DiMaggio and Mickey Mantle. He batted over .300 eight times in a row.

ABOVE: Reggie Jackson   **RIGHT**: Jorge Posada

JORGE POSADA   Catcher

- BORN: 8/17/1971
- PLAYED FOR TEAM: 1995 TO 2011

Jorge Posada was a switch-hitter with a powerful batting stroke. He was an All-Star five times. Only Yogi Berra hit more home runs than Posada as a catcher for the Yankees.

MARIANO RIVERA   Pitcher

- BORN: 11/29/1969   • FIRST YEAR WITH TEAM: 1995

Mariano Rivera became baseball's best relief pitcher with the Yankees. He set the team record for **saves** with 50 in 2001.

DEREK JETER   Shortstop

- BORN: 6/26/1974   • FIRST YEAR WITH TEAM: 1995

Derek Jeter became one of the best all-around players the Yankees ever had. He was the **Rookie of the Year** in 1996 and won five Gold Gloves from 2004 to 2010.

ROBINSON CANO   Second Baseman

- BORN: 10/22/1982   • FIRST YEAR WITH TEAM: 2005

Robinson Cano was named after another famous second baseman, Jackie Robinson. Like him, Cano began his career in a big way. He batted .342 in his second season and quickly became one of baseball's top hitters.

CALLING THE SHOTS

The first manager to lead the Yankees to a championship was Miller Huggins. New York won three World Series under Huggins. Joe McCarthy had even greater success. He managed the Yankees from 1931 to 1946. The team won seven World Series, including four in a row from 1936 to 1939. McCarthy was a good teacher and a master at the *strategy* of baseball.

Three years after McCarthy left the team, Casey Stengel came aboard in 1949. He was also a clever manager, but he often confused people with the strange way he explained things. People began to see he was a baseball genius when the Yankees won the World Series in each of his first five seasons. The team won two more before Stengel retired.

JOE GIRARDI
Mgr. New York Yankees®

Starting in the 1970s, the person calling the shots in New York was the team's owner, George Steinbrenner. He believed the Yankees should win every year. Steinbrenner's managers wanted to win as badly as he did. Often they argued with him. Billy Martin led the Yankees to pennants in 1976 and 1977. Even so, Steinbrenner fired him in 1978. Then he rehired Martin three more times!

The manager who worked best with Steinbrenner was Joe Torre. He was always very calm. Torre won the World Series in 1996, his first season in New York. During his 12 years as manager, the team went to the playoffs every fall and won four championships. In 2008, Joe Girardi took over as manager. He had been a catcher for Torre and also a coach. Girardi led the Yankees to their 27th championship in 2009.

ONE GREAT DAY

The best a pitcher can do in a nine-inning game is face 27 batters and get 27 outs. This is called a "perfect game." In the last 100 years, fewer than 20 pitchers have thrown a perfect game. When Don Larsen delivered the first pitch in Game 5 of the 1956 World Series, no one in Yankee Stadium thought they would be witnessing perfection that day.

Larsen was not New York's best pitcher. He had a good fastball, but the Brooklyn Dodgers had already hit him hard in Game 2. They could hardly wait to face him a second time. To their surprise, Larsen got them to ground out, fly out, or strike out inning after inning. Not a single Dodger made it to first base. The closest thing to a hit was a line drive by Gil Hodges to left-center field. Mickey Mantle caught the ball after a long run.

In the ninth inning, with the Yankees winning 2–0, Larsen took a deep breath and went to work. The first batter, Carl Furillo, fouled off four pitches before flying out. The second batter, Roy Campanella,

ABOVE: Don Larsen delivers a pitch against the Brooklyn Dodgers.
INSET: His perfect game in the 1956 World Series was front-page news.

grounded out to second base. The third man up was Dale Mitchell, a pinch-hitting specialist who was batting for the pitcher. Larsen got two strikes on Mitchell.

With everyone in Yankee Stadium on their feet, Larsen threw a fastball on the outside corner and umpire Babe Pinelli called it strike three. The game was over. Catcher Yogi Berra popped out of his crouch and jumped into Larsen's arms. No one could believe what they had just seen. As one newspaper put it the next day, "The imperfect man had pitched a perfect game."

LEGEND HAS IT

IS AUGUST THE YANKEES' FAVORITE MONTH?

LEGEND HAS IT that it is. While many teams fade in the heat of August, the

Yankees usually play very well during this month. In 1998, when New York won 114 games, the team had 22 victories in August. In 1938, the Yankees had their best August ever. When the month began, they held a slim lead over the second-place team. New York won 28 times that August. At the end of the month they were ahead by 14 games!

ABOVE: Lou Gehrig and Joe DiMaggio combined for 16 homers and 82 RBIs in August of 1938.

WHICH YANKEE WAS THE BEST PERFORMER OFF THE FIELD?

LEGEND HAS IT that Bernie Williams was the most artistic Yankee. Many Yankees have had parts in movies, including Babe Ruth, Lou Gehrig, and Mickey Mantle. George Steinbrenner acted in beer and credit card commercials. Derek Jeter once hosted the TV show *Saturday Night Live*. But Williams wins for his wonderful CDs *The Journey Within* and *Moving Forward*. They feature Williams playing the guitar. Few fans realized that he gave up a career in music for a career in baseball at the age of 16.

DID BABE RUTH PREDICT HIS OWN HOME RUN IN THE 1932 WORLD SERIES?

LEGEND HAS IT that he did. Batting against the Chicago Cubs in Wrigley Field, Ruth was being booed by the fans and insulted by the Chicago players. After pitcher Charlie Root threw a strike, Ruth held up one finger. When Root threw a second strike, Ruth held up two fingers. Then he pointed to center field and said something that no one could hear. Ruth hit the next pitch into the center field stands and rounded the bases with a big smile on his face. Ruth claimed he "called" his home run. The Cubs claimed he did not. No one will ever know for sure.

IT REALLY HAPPENED

The last player to bat .400 in a season was Ted Williams of the Boston Red Sox in 1941. Williams won the batting championship that year and also led the league in runs scored and home runs. However, the talk of baseball in 1941 was not Williams. It was Joe DiMaggio of the Yankees.

On May 15, DiMaggio cracked four hits against the Chicago White Sox. He hit a triple and a home run the following day, and then a single the day after that. On June 13, the Yankees returned from a long road trip. By this time, baseball fans were starting to get excited about DiMaggio. Since that May afternoon four weeks earlier, he had gotten at least one hit in every game. His streak stood at 26 games in a row.

That summer, Americans had a lot of worries. The **Great Depression** had not yet ended. In Europe and Asia, war had broken out. People needed something fun to think about. As June turned to July, everyone had the same question at the end of each day: "Did Joe get a hit today?" The answer was always *Yes*.

Joe DiMaggio poses for a photo in the spring of 1941.

DiMaggio broke the AL record of 41 games in a row on June 29. He broke the all-time record of 44 games on July 2, right before the All-Star Game. Finally, on July 17—more than two months after he started—the Cleveland Indians stopped DiMaggio's streak at 56 games. It took a couple of great fielding plays by third baseman Ken Keltner to do it.

The next day, "Joltin' Joe" picked right up where he had left off. DiMaggio smashed a single and a double against Cleveland. This time his hitting streak reached "only" 16 games.

TEAM SPIRIT

When the Yankees are down, they love to hear their fans cheer them to victory. In the days following the terror attacks of September 11, 2001, New York City was down. There was great sadness in the streets. Some people asked whether it was even worth playing the rest of the baseball season.

That fall, the Yankees reminded New Yorkers how important baseball was to the city's spirit. After losing the first two games of the World Series in Arizona, the Yankees returned home and won three games in a row. Each time, they battled back from behind. New Yorkers began to feel good about themselves and their city again. Thanks to the Yankees, they realized that everyone gets knocked down in life, but it takes pride and courage to get back up again.

LEFT: Derek Jeter signs a ball for a young fan.
ABOVE: New York fans show their spirit during the 2001 World Series.

TIMELINE

Fans bought this program on Opening Day in 1923.

1901
The team plays its first season as the Baltimore Orioles.

1923
Yankee Stadium opens.

1941
Joe DiMaggio hits in 56 straight games.

1903
The team moves to New York and becomes the Highlanders.

1927
Babe Ruth hits 60 home runs.

1939
Lou Gehrig plays in his 2,130th game in a row.

Jack Chesbro led the 1903 team with 21 wins.

This card celebrates Babe Ruth's home run record.

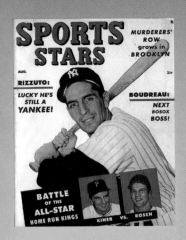

Phil Rizzuto was a team leader all through the 1950s.

Don Mattingly

1953
The Yankees win their fifth World Series in a row.

1985
Don Mattingly is named MVP.

2011
Derek Jeter gets his 3,000th hit.

1961
Roger Maris breaks Babe Ruth's record with 61 home runs.

1977
Reggie Jackson hits three home runs in Game 6 of the World Series.

2007
Alex Rodriguez wins his second MVP as a Yankee.

Alex Rodriguez

Fun Facts

What a Relief

In 2011, Mariano Rivera became baseball's all-time leader in saves. The Yankees have a long tradition of great relief pitchers, including Johnny Murphy, Joe Page, Sparky Lyle, Goose Gossage, and Dave Righetti.

Fit to Print

Although the team didn't officially change its name until 1913, some New York newspapers had been using the name "Yankees" for years. The name "Highlanders" was often too long to fit in a newspaper headline.

Numbers Game

The Yankees were the first baseball team to "retire" the numbers of famous players. Once a number is retired, it cannot be worn again.

COWBOY LOU

During the 1930s, everyone loved cowboy movies. In 1938, Lou Gehrig played a cowboy in *Rawhide*. In one scene, he defends himself from bad guys by throwing billiard balls at them.

LUCKY 13

In 2010, Alex Rodriguez had 30 homers and more than 100 **runs batted in (RBIs)** for the Yankees. He was the first player ever to have "30–100" seasons 13 years in a row. Rodriguez's uniform number is also 13!

SWEET

Reggie Jackson once joked that if he played in New York, a candy bar would be named after him. In 1977, Jackson signed with the Yankees. A few months later, the REGGIE! bar was in candy stores across America.

LEFT: Sparky Lyle was the league's best pitcher in 1977.
ABOVE: Lou Gehrig puts on movie makeup for a scene in *Rawhide*.

Talking Baseball

"It ain't over until it's over."

▶ **YOGI BERRA**, *ON WHY THE YANKEES NEVER GIVE UP*

"He has it in his body to be great."

▶ **CASEY STENGEL**, *ON MICKEY MANTLE*

"I swing big, with everything I've got. I hit big or I miss big. I like to live as big as I can."

▶ **BABE RUTH**, *ON HIS LOVE OF BASEBALL AND LIFE*

"A good catcher is the quarterback … the lead dog … the traffic cop and sometimes a lot of unprintable things, but no team gets very far without one."

▶ **MILLER HUGGINS**, *ON THE IMPORTANCE OF A CATCHER TO HIS TEAM*

"Here, you have to win."

▶ **DEREK JETER**, *ON THE PRESSURE OF PLAYING FOR THE YANKEES*

"There is no room in baseball for discrimination. It is our national **pastime** and a game for all."

▶ **LOU GEHRIG**, *ON THE RULE THAT BARRED AFRICAN-AMERICANS FROM BASEBALL WHEN HE PLAYED*

"I get the ball, I throw the ball, and then I take a shower."

▶ **MARIANO RIVERA**, *ON THE LIFE OF A SUPERSTAR RELIEF PITCHER*

"New Yorkers are strong people. You have to give the city a team that's filled with battlers."

▶ **GEORGE STEINBRENNER**, *ON THE WAY HE LIKED TO BUILD A TEAM*

"I'm just a ballplayer with one *ambition*, and that is to give all I've got to help my ball club win."

▶ **JOE DIMAGGIO**, *ON HOW HE STAYED SO FOCUSED ON THE FIELD*

LEFT: Yogi Berra   **ABOVE**: Derek Jeter

39

GREAT DEBATES

People who root for the Yankees love to compare their favorite moments, teams, and players. Some debates have been going on for years! How would you settle these classic baseball arguments?

ROBINSON CANO IS THE BEST SECOND BASEMAN IN TEAM HISTORY ...

... because he could hit, field, run, and throw as well as anyone the Yankees ever had. Cano (LEFT) hit for a high average and had tremendous power. In a lineup with Derek Jeter, Alex Rodrgiuez, and Curtis Granderson, Cano was the batter other teams were most afraid to face. When he got hot, it was almost impossible to cool him down.

NOT SO FAST. HE'LL HAVE TO GET IN LINE BEHIND JOE GORDON AND TONY LAZZERI FOR NOW ...

... because they are both Hall of Famers. Gordon was good for 20 homers and 100 RBIs almost every year. He was the MVP in 1942 and an All-Star in each of his seven seasons in New York. Lazzeri hit the ball even harder than Gordon. He knocked in 100 runs seven times. Lazzeri still holds the team record with 12 RBIs in one game!

THE HOME RUN BY CHRIS CHAMBLISS IN THE 1976 PLAYOFFS WAS THE MOST THRILLING HIT IN YANKEE STADIUM HISTORY ...

... because it won the pennant. The Yankees hadn't been to the World Series since 1964. They were playing in the final game of the **American League Championship Series (ALCS)**. Chambliss blasted a pitch over the right field fence and practically had to fight his way around the bases. Thousands of people rushed on the field to congratulate him. Everyone in Yankee Stadium had goose bumps!

MICKEY MANTLE'S MONSTER SHOT IN 1963 WAS THE ULTIMATE GOOSE-BUMP MOMENT ...

... because the people who saw it still can't believe their eyes. In the game that spring, Mantle (RIGHT) hit a ball that kept going and going. It soared on a line to right field and clanked off the Yankee Stadium *facade*. Fans say the ball was still rising at the time. Mantle barely missed being the only player to hit a fair ball out of Yankee Stadium. Had it cleared the roof, some experts believe it would have traveled close to 600 feet. Mantle said it was the hardest ball he ever hit.

FOR THE RECORD

The great Yankees teams and players have left their marks on the record books. These are the "best of the best" ...

YANKEES AWARD WINNERS

WINNER	AWARD	YEAR	WINNER	AWARD	YEAR
Lou Gehrig	MVP	1936	Thurman Munson	MVP	1976
Joe DiMaggio	MVP	1939	Sparky Lyle	Cy Young Award	1977
Joe DiMaggio	MVP	1941	Ron Guidry	Cy Young Award	1978
Joe Gordon	MVP	1942	Dave Righetti	Rookie of the Year	1981
Spud Chandler	MVP	1943	Don Mattingly	MVP	1985
Joe DiMaggio	MVP	1947	Buck Showalter	Manager of the Year	1994
Phil Rizzuto	MVP	1950	Joe Torre	Manager of the Year	1996
Gil McDougald	Rookie of the Year	1951	Derek Jeter	Rookie of the Year	1996
Yogi Berra	MVP	1951	Joe Torre	Manager of the Year	1998
Bob Grim	Rookie of the Year	1954	Roger Clemens	Cy Young Award	2001
Yogi Berra	MVP	1954	Alex Rodriguez	MVP	2005
Yogi Berra	MVP	1955	Alex Rodriguez	MVP	2007
Mickey Mantle	MVP	1956			
Tony Kubek	Rookie of the Year	1957			
Mickey Mantle	MVP	1957			
Bob Turley	Cy Young Award	1958			
Roger Maris	MVP	1960			
Whitey Ford	Cy Young Award	1961			
Roger Maris	MVP	1961			
Tom Tresh	Rookie of the Year	1962			
Mickey Mantle	MVP	1962			
Elston Howard	MVP	1963			
Stan Bahnsen	Rookie of the Year	1968			
Thurman Munson	Rookie of the Year	1970			

Elston Howard won the MVP in 1963 and was an All-Star nine years in a row.

YANKEES ACHIEVEMENTS

ACHIEVEMENT	YEAR	ACHIEVEMENT	YEAR
AL Pennant Winner	1921	AL Pennant Winner	1953
AL Pennant Winner	1922	World Series Champions	1953
AL Pennant Winner	1923	AL Pennant Winner	1955
World Series Champions	1923	AL Pennant Winner	1956
AL Pennant Winner	1926	World Series Champions	1956
AL Pennant Winner	1927	AL Pennant Winner	1957
World Series Champions	1927	AL Pennant Winner	1958
AL Pennant Winner	1928	World Series Champions	1958
World Series Champions	1928	AL Pennant Winner	1960
AL Pennant Winner	1932	AL Pennant Winner	1961
World Series Champions	1932	World Series Champions	1961
AL Pennant Winner	1936	AL Pennant Winner	1962
World Series Champions	1936	World Series Champions	1962
AL Pennant Winner	1937	AL Pennant Winner	1963
World Series Champions	1937	AL Pennant Winner	1964
AL Pennant Winner	1938	AL Pennant Winner	1976
World Series Champions	1938	AL Pennant Winner	1977
AL Pennant Winner	1939	World Series Champions	1977
World Series Champions	1939	AL Pennant Winner	1978
AL Pennant Winner	1941	World Series Champions	1978
World Series Champions	1941	AL Pennant Winner	1981
AL Pennant Winner	1942	AL Pennant Winner	1996
AL Pennant Winner	1943	World Series Champions	1996
World Series Champions	1943	AL Pennant Winner	1998
AL Pennant Winner	1947	World Series Champions	1998
World Series Champions	1947	AL Pennant Winner	1999
AL Pennant Winner	1949	World Series Champions	1999
World Series Champions	1949	AL Pennant Winner	2000
AL Pennant Winner	1950	World Series Champions	2000
World Series Champions	1950	AL Pennant Winner	2001
AL Pennant Winner	1951	AL Pennant Winner	2003
World Series Champions	1951	AL Pennant Winner	2009
AL Pennant Winner	1952	World Series Champions	2009
World Series Champions	1952		

PINPOINTS

The history of a baseball team is made up of many smaller stories. These stories take place all over the map—not just in the city a team calls "home." Match the pushpins on these maps to the **TEAM FACTS**, and you will begin to see the story of the Yankees unfold!

1 Baltimore, Maryland—*The team played here in 1901 and 1902.*

2 New York City, New York—*The team has played here since 1903.*

3 Pequannock, New Jersey—*Derek Jeter was born here.*

4 Evansville, Indiana—*Don Mattingly was born here.*

5 St. Louis, Missouri—*Yogi Berra was born here.*

6 Hibbing, Minnesota—*Roger Maris was born here.*

7 Commerce, Oklahoma—*Mickey Mantle was born here.*

8 Lafayette, Louisiana—*Ron Guidry was born here.*

9 Martinez, California—*Joe DiMaggio was born here.*

10 San Juan, Puerto Rico—*Bernie Williams was born here.*

11 Panama City, Panama—*Mariano Rivera was born here.*

12 Ishikawa, Japan—*Hideki Matsui was born here.*

Bernie Williams

GLOSSARY

BASEBALL WORDS
VOCABULARY WORDS

ALL-STAR—A player who is selected to play in baseball's annual All-Star Game.

AMERICAN LEAGUE CHAMPIONSHIP SERIES (ALCS)—The playoff series that has decided the American League pennant since 1969.

AMBITION—Desire to succeed.

AMERICAN LEAGUE (AL)—One of baseball's two major leagues; the AL began play in 1901.

CATHEDRAL—A large church.

CLUTCH—Pressure situations.

CY YOUNG AWARD—The award given each year to each league's best pitcher.

DECADE—A period of 10 years; also specific periods, such as the 1950s.

FACADE—The front of a building.

FREE AGENTS—Players who are allowed to join any team that wants them.

GOLD GLOVES—The awards given each year to baseball's best fielders.

GREAT DEPRESSION—The economic crisis that started in 1929 and lasted until the 1940s.

HALL OF FAME—The museum in Cooperstown, New York, where baseball's greatest players are honored. A player voted into the Hall of Fame is sometimes called a "Hall of Famer."

LOGO—A symbol or design that represents a company or team.

MAJESTIC—Grand or spectacular.

MINOR LEAGUES—The many professional leagues that help develop players for the major leagues.

MOST VALUABLE PLAYER (MVP)—The award given each year to each league's top player; an MVP is also selected for the World Series and the All-Star Game.

PASTIME—Something that gives people pleasure.

PENNANT—A league championship. The term comes from the triangular flag awarded to each season's champion, beginning in the 1870s.

PINSTRIPES—Thin stripes.

PLAYOFFS—The games played after the regular season to determine which teams will advance to the World Series.

POSTSEASON—The games played after the regular season, including the playoffs and World Series.

ROLE PLAYERS—Players who do specific things to help their team.

ROOKIE OF THE YEAR—The annual award given to each league's best first-year player.

RUNS BATTED IN (RBIs)—A statistic that counts the number of runners a batter drives home.

SAVES—A statistic that counts the number of times a relief pitcher finishes off a close victory for his team.

STRATEGY—A plan or method for succeeding.

SWITCH-HITTER—A player who can hit from either side of home plate.

TRADITION—A belief or custom that is handed down from generation to generation.

WORLD SERIES—The world championship series played between the American League and National League pennant winners.

WORLD WAR II—The war between the major powers of Europe, Asia, and North America that lasted from 1939 to 1945. The United States entered the war in 1941.

EXTRA INNINGS

TEAM SPIRIT introduces a great way to stay up to date with your team! Visit our **EXTRA INNINGS** link and get connected to the latest and greatest updates. **EXTRA INNINGS** serves as a young reader's ticket to an exclusive web page—with more stories, fun facts, team records, and photos of the Yankees. Content is updated during and after each season. The **EXTRA INNINGS** feature also enables readers to send comments and letters to the author! Log onto: **www.norwoodhousepress.com/library.aspx** and click on the tab: **TEAM SPIRIT** to access **EXTRA INNINGS**.

Read all the books in the series to learn more about professional sports. For a complete listing of the baseball, basketball, football, and hockey teams in the **TEAM SPIRIT** series, visit our website at: **www.norwoodhousepress.com/library.aspx**

ON THE ROAD

NEW YORK YANKEES
One East 161st Street
Bronx, New York 10451
(718) 293-4300
newyork.yankees.mlb.com

NATIONAL BASEBALL
HALL OF FAME AND MUSEUM
25 Main Street
Cooperstown, New York 13326
(888) 425-5633
www.baseballhalloffame.org

ON THE BOOKSHELF

To learn more about the sport of baseball, look for these books at your library or bookstore:

* Augustyn, Adam (editor). *The Britannica Guide to Baseball.* New York, NY: Rosen Publishing, 2011.

* Dreier, David. *Baseball: How It Works.* North Mankato, MN: Capstone Press, 2010.

* Stewart, Mark. *Ultimate 10: Baseball.* New York, NY: Gareth Stevens Publishing, 2009.

INDEX

PAGE NUMBERS IN **BOLD** REFER TO ILLUSTRATIONS.

Bahnsen, Stan 42
Berra, Yogi **8**, 9, 17, 21,
       23, 27, 38, **38**, 42, 45
Boggs, Wade 11
Caldwell, Slim 6
Campanella, Roy 26
Cano, Robinson 11, 19, 23, 40, **40**
Chambliss, Chris 18, 41
Chandler, Spud 17, 42
Chesbro, Jack 6, **34**
Clemens, Roger 11, 42
Combs, Earle 7, 16, **16**
Dickey, Bill 7, **15**, 16
DiMaggio, Joe 7, **7**, 17, 21, 22, **28**,
       30, 31, **31**, 34, 39, 42, 45
Ford, Russ 6
Ford, Whitey 9, 17, 21, **21**, 42
Furillo, Carl 26
Gehrig, Lou 7, **7**, 16, 20, **20**,
       28, 29, 34, 37, **37**, 39, 42
Giambi, Jason 11
Girardi, Joe 25, **25**
Gomez, Lefty 7, **7**, 17, **17**
Gordon, Joe 16, 21, 40, 42
Gossage, Goose 18, 36
Granderson, Curtis 40
Grim, Bob 42
Guidry, Ron 18, 42, 45
Henrich, Tommy 16
Hodges, Gil 26
Howard, Elston 9, 17, 42, **42**
Hoyt, Waite 16
Huggins, Miller 24, **24**, 38
Jackson, Reggie 9, 18,
       22, **22**, 35, 37
Jeter, Derek 10, **10**, 11, 19, 23,
       29, **32**, 35, 39, **39**, 40, 42, 45
Keller, Charlie 16
Keltner, Ken 31
Kubek, Tony 42
Larsen, Don 26, 27, **27**
Lazzeri, Tony 7, **7**, 16, 40
Lopat, Eddie 17
Lyle, Sparky 36, **36**, 42
Mantle, Mickey 7, **8**, 9, 17, 21,
       22, 26, 29, 38, 41, **41**, 42, 45
Maris, Roger 9, 17, 35, 42, 45
Martin, Billy 17, 25
Martinez, Tino 10

Matsui, Hideki 11, 15, 45
Mattingly, Don 10, 22,
       35, **35**, 42, 45
McCarthy, Joe 24
McDougald, Gil 42
Meusel, Bob 7, 16, **16**
Mitchell, Dale 27
Munson, Thurman 9, 18, **18**, 22, 42
Murphy, Johnny 17, 36
Mussina, Mike 11
Nettles, Graig 18
O'Neill, Paul 10, 19
Page, Joe 17, 36
Pennock, Herb 16
Pettitte, Andy 10, 11, 19
Pinelli, Babe 27
Piniella, Lou 18
Posada, Jorge 10, 11, 19, 23, **23**
Randolph, Willie 18
Raschi, Vic 17
Reynolds, Allie 17
Richardson, Bobby 17
Righetti, Dave 10, 36, 42
Rivera, Mariano 10, 11, **11**,
       19, 23, 36, 39, 45
Rivers, Mickey 18
Rizzuto, Phil 9, 17, **35**, 42
Robinson, Jackie 23
Rodriguez, Alex 11, 19, 35,
       35, 37, 40, 42
Root, Charlie 29
Ruffing, Red 7, 17
Ruth, Babe 6, **6**, 7, 9, 16,
       16, 20, 29, 34, **34**, 35, 38
Sabathia, CC 11, **14**, 19
Shawkey, Bob 16
Showalter, Buck 42
Skowron, Bill 17
Soriano, Alfonso 10
Steinbrenner, George 9, **9**, 25, 29, 39
Stengel, Casey 24, 38
Teixeira, Mark 11, 19
Torre, Joe **9**, 10, 25, 42
Tresh, Tom 42
Turley, Bob 17, 42
Williams, Bernie 10, 19,
       22, 29, 45, **45**
Williams, Ted 30
Winfield, Dave 10

ABOUT THE AUTHOR

MARK STEWART has written more than 50 books on baseball and over 150 sports books for kids. He grew up in New York City during the 1960s rooting for the Yankees and Mets, and was lucky enough to meet players from both teams. Mark comes from a family of writers. His grandfather was Sunday Editor of *The New York Times,* and his mother was Articles Editor of *Ladies' Home Journal* and *McCall's.* Mark has profiled hundreds of athletes over the past 25 years. He has also written several books about his native New York and New Jersey, his home today. Mark is a graduate of Duke University, with a degree in history. He lives and works in a home overlooking Sandy Hook, New Jersey. You can contact Mark through the Norwood House Press website.